ROSES

JANET BROWNE

A ROMANTIC HISTORY WITH A GUIDE TO CULTIVATION

RUNNING PRESS
Philadelphia, Pennsylvania

Copyright © 1992 by Inklink

Concept, design & editorial direction Simon Jennings.
Produced, edited, and designed by Inklink,
Greenwich, London, England.

Text by Janet Browne
Designed by Simon Jennings & Alan Marshall
Edited by Peter Leek
Instructional illustrations by Robin Harris

Published in The United States of America
by Running Press, Philadelphia, Pennsylvania

Text setting and computer make-up by Inklink, London.
Image generation by Blackheath Publishing Services, London.
Printed in Hong Kong.

Canadian representatives: General Publishing Co., Ltd.,
30 Lesmill Road, Don Mills, Ontario M3B 2T6.
International representatives: Worldwide Media Services, Inc.,
115 East Twenty-Third Street, New York, New York 10010.

9 8 7 6 5 4 3 2 1
Digit on the right indicates the number of this printing.

Library of Congress Catalog Number 91-50910

ISBN 1-56138-088-1

This book may be ordered by mail from the publisher.
Please add $2.50 for postage and handling.
But try your bookstore first!
Running Press Book Publishers
125 South Twenty-Second Street
Philadelphia, Pennsylvania 19103

ROSES

A ROMANTIC HISTORY
WITH A GUIDE TO CULTIVATION
ARRANGED IN FOUR CHAPTERS

CONTENTS

THE ROSE
Queen of Flowers
"A lovely being, scarcely form'd or moulded,
A rose with all its sweetest leaves yet folded."
FROM "DON JUAN" BY LORD BYRON (1788-1824)

Introduction

No one who loves flowers can fail to be captivated by the gorgeous colors, velvet texture, subtle fragrance, and perfect shape of the rose. Fittingly honored by the ancient Greeks as "the Queen of Flowers," the rose has since the earliest times been one of the best loved and most commonly cultivated garden plants. No doubt the natural beauty and fragrance of the flower has been responsible for this fascination, but the rose has always been surrounded by a special mystique and it has played a unique role in human lives and history.

Today the beauty of the rose is widely appreciated, and rose breeders throughout the world continually strive to produce improved or new and unusual varieties for our delight – as rosarians have patiently been doing since as long ago as 5000 BC.

The uses to which roses may be put are remarkably varied – ranging from large garden displays to a single bud in a buttonhole, from rose oil to crystalized petals, from herbal medicine to potpourri and perfumes. They have also been used for winemaking and cooking, as subject matter for romantic paintings, songs, and poems, as religious symbols and heraldic emblems.

As well as explaining how modern roses have been bred and how they are classified, the book includes practical advice about rose growing – so that the many forms of this lovely plant may be enjoyed to the fullest and our appreciation of it never diminish.

DEDICATED TO
OUR ENVIRONMENT
WHICH SUFFERS
IN SILENCE

CHAPTER

I

ROSES IN HISTORY

I SOMETIMES THINK THAT NEVER BLOWS SO RED
THE ROSE AS WHERE SOME BURIED CAESAR BLED
FROM "THE RUBAIYAT" OF OMAR KHAYYAM c. 1050-1123

THE FIRST ROSES

ARCHAEOLOGISTS HAVE DISCOVERED FOSSILIZED ROSES that may be as old as 30 million years. These have all been found in the Northern Hemisphere, and it is now thought that originally roses only occurred north of the equator (probably because they require cool conditions to germinate and grow well), while those found south of the equator must have been taken there by man.

The first known paintings of roses are to be found in the Palace of Knossos in Crete, which dates back to 1800-1700 BC. When the frescoes were restored after an earthquake around 1400 BC, the restorers painted the roses with six petals instead of five, which caused some confusion as to the identity of the plant when the frescoes were unearthed. Later, part of the original frescoes was discovered undamaged, and there could be no doubt that the pink five-petalled flowers were indeed those of the wild rose.

In Egyptian tombs of around 1500 BC, roses have been found as decorations, along with other ornaments and artifacts. Also, clay tablets record their existence beyond doubt as part of the Egyptian way of life at that time.

The first written record mentioning roses dates from about 5000 BC, when the Sumerians lived in the fertile part of Mesopotamia that is now Iraq. Discovered in the royal tombs at Ur by the British archaeologist Sir Leonard Woolley, the tablets were made of soft clay and had been well preserved. The writing on them was done with a plant stalk such as a reed.

Perhaps the most famous ancient work of literature that mentions roses is *The Iliad*, the Greek poet Homer's epic account of the siege of Troy (c. 1205 BC). Homer relates that Achilles' shield was decorated with roses in celebration of his victory over Hector, and that Hector's body was annointed with rose oil before it was embalmed.

10

THE ANCESTOR OF ALL ROSES

R. GALLICA is the ancestor of most old European roses, and would have been familiar to gardeners in the ancient world.
From A COLLECTION OF ROSES FROM NATURE by Mary Lawrence, 1799.

Rosa Gallica.   *Red Officinal Rose.*

References to roses also occur in the writings of the Greek historian Herodotus (c.485-425 BC). He mentions that when Midas, the deposed King of the Phrygians, moved westwards to Macedonia, he took with him fragrant roses that had sixty petals. Experts have suggested that these were double forms of *Rosa gallica*, an ancestor of many present-day roses. If so, these would have been an example of natural mutation — and it is known that as roses were transplanted from place to place and from country to country, more and more variations occurred. As a result, many of the early roses were given names such as 'The Rose of Paestum' (Italy), 'The Rose of Miletus' (Turkey), and 'The Rose of Rhodes' (Greece), although all three were probably forms of *R. gallica*.

11

EARLY CULTIVATION

THE GREEK PHILOSOPHER THEOPHRASTUS (c. 372-286 BC) may well have been the first person to make a botanical study of plants, or at least the first to write about taking cuttings. "The rose and the lily," he notes, "are generated when the stems are cut up . . . The rose also grows from seed." He goes on to mention that roses can be propagated by budding, and lists the wild roses collected from the Macedonian mountains.

Other European authors of those early days also referred specifically and enthusiastically to roses. It is apparent that the plants played a prominent role in the lives of the people of Egypt, Greece, and Italy of that time. In fact, so financially rewarding was it to grow roses that Greek and Roman farmers cultivated them as field crops. Indeed, the Roman poet Horace (65-8 BC) complained that too many roses were being grown in Italy and not enough corn – a sentiment echoed by another Roman poet, Martial, several decades later. Just how important the flowers were to the Romans is illustrated by the fact that Pliny the Elder (AD 23-79) devoted a whole chapter to roses and their cultivation in his encyclopedic work *Historia Naturalis*, written in AD 77.

The emperor and the rose
The use of roses by the Romans as a symbol of luxury and opulence reached new heights of excess under the Emperor Nero.

In ancient Rome roses seem to have been associated with practically every aspect of life – particularly romance, spectacle, and intrigue. Politicians, for example, used to hang roses from the ceiling to indicate that a meeting was secret – hence the term *sub rosa*. As for romance – and sheer extravagance – it was said that Cleopatra greeted her lover, Mark Antony, in a room knee-deep in rose petals, that they sat on petal-filled mattresses, wore rose garlands, and had containers filled with rose oil for added fragrance. Although the Romans had discovered how to cultivate roses in heated glasshouses to provide winter flowers, the Egyptians did a brisk trade in exporting the blooms throughout the year. The rich were thus able to indulge their passion for roses for all celebratory occasions. Not only were the petals used for perfumed baths and scented sachets, at banquets the floor was carpeted with roses, and crowns of roses were presented to victorious warriors. They also featured in funerary rites (before committing suicide, Mark Antony requested that his tomb should be covered with roses); and they were used for culinary and medicinal purposes, too.

The Emperor Nero, in particular, is reputed to have spent vast sums of money on banquets where masses of roses were employed to create a luxurious ambience and rose-water baths were freely available. On one occasion, a number of guests were even said to have been suffocated by the weight of rose petals released into the air. In fact, according to some historians of the time, Nero was so lavish in his use of roses that his extravagance contributed to the collapse of the Roman Empire.

Although most early European literature refers to roses grown in the Mediterranian region, roses had long been popular in Persia (Iran), where in the sixth century BC King Kyros II adopted the rose as his royal emblem. And in what is now Iraq, the hanging gardens of Babylon – which were begun by King Nebuchadnezzar around 1200 BC and became one of the seven wonders of the ancient world – were almost certainly planted with roses to satisfy his wife's love of the flowers.

Omar Khayyam, the famous eleventh-century Persian poet, frequently mentions roses in his poems, as did the thirteenth-century poet Sadi. There is also the delightful Persian story of the "Duel of the Roses," recorded by the poet Nizami in the twelfth century. This tells of a contest between two physicians, each intent on outwitting the other. The more cunning of the two saves himself from being poisoned by swallowing an antidote, then makes his rival smell a rose over which he has cast a fatal spell.

13

THE SPREAD OF THE ROSE

Roses were also being grown widely in China. Indeed, according to the philosopher and sage Confucius (551-479 BC) the Imperial Museum contained no fewer than 600 books on roses.

Gradually, as the centuries passed, roses were introduced into more and more countries, until by the fifteenth century they were being grown in most areas where the climate and soil were suitable. They were taken to America by the first of the Pilgrim Fathers, and in 1620 Edward Winslow reported that in Massachusetts there was "an abundance of roses, white, red and damask, single but very sweet indeed."

With the invention of the printing press in 1440, many rose books were translated and others written, which helped publicize the rose still further. One of the most useful books was John Gerard's *Herball*, published in 1597. A plant lover who held the rose in high esteem, he described and illustrated eighteen wild and garden roses in the first edition and added more in the second. Other early botanical and gardening authors who devote space to roses include Carolus Clusius, Emanuel Sweerts, John Parkinson, Linnaeus, and Philip Miller, who in the eighteenth century recorded twenty-six roses. Nurseries had also begun to compile catalogs of roses, among them Lee & Kennedy who in 1744 listed forty-four different kinds.

Early rose engravings from the FLORILEGIUM by Emanuel Sweerts, 1612

WILD ROSES

By the end of the eighteenth century more and more roses were being noted, and it was becoming obvious to botanists that, although the apparent diversity could partly be attributed to mistaken identity, clearly some wild species of the genus *Rosa* had hybridized naturally or crossed with each other randomly to create new varieties. To help sort out the confusion, in 1949 the American botanist Alfred Rehder devised a classification of four sub-genera for all wild roses – a scheme that is followed to a large extent today.

Rehder classified the majority of wild roses under the sub-genus *Eurosa*, which he divided into ten sections:

PIMPINELLIFOLIAE – Europe & Asia
GALLICANAE – France
CANINAE – Europe, North Africa, & Western Asia
CAROLINAE – North America
CINNAMOMEAE – Eastern Asia, Europe, & North America
SYNSTYLAE – mainly Eastern Asia but including *R. setigera*, the 'Prairie Rose' of North America
CHINENSIS (syn. INDICAE) – China
BANKSIANAE – China
LAEVIGATAE – China
BRACTEATAE – South-East Asia.

R. BANKSIAE LUTEA

The characteristics of these ten groups reveal that deep-yellow roses grow wild only in Asia; deep-red wild roses are found only in China; and that the very few wild roses that flower twice in a season all come from Eastern Asia.

The three other sub-genera distinguished by Rehder, which consisted of very simplified roses, were:

Hulthemia
(one species, *R. persica*, found in Iran & Pakistan)
Hesperrhodos
(three species found in the south & west of the U.S.A.)
Platyrhodon
(one species, *R. roxburghii*, found in China & Japan).

15

Natural habitats

THE WILD-ROSE SPECIES KNOWN TODAY grow mainly in the Northern Hemisphere, where the fossilized remains of early roses were found. They occur as far north as Alaska and Siberia, in north and central Asia, in parts of Europe and North Africa, throughout North America, and as far south as Mexico. As mentioned earlier, rose seeds need a cool period in order to germinate – and all these areas have at least some spells of cold weather.

Wild-rose habitats
The broad tinted band shows the natural habitats of the wild rose.

Growing conditions

Wild roses generally prefer well-drained upland sites where there is not too much competition from other plants. However, R. PALUSTRIS (the Swamp Rose) is found in marshy ground in America and Canada; R. STELLATA thrives in the mountains of New Mexico; and R. ACICULARIS (right) in the Arctic.

R. ACICULARIS (ARCTIC ROSE)

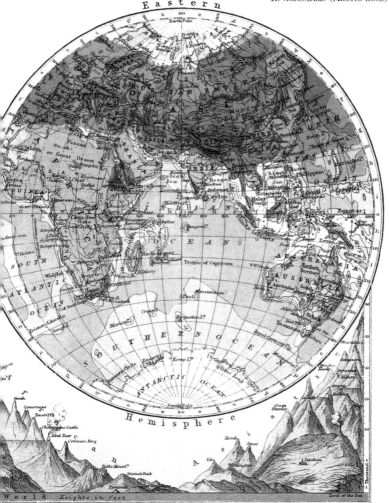

17

EARLY ROSE GARDENS

THE FIRST FORMAL GARDENS containing roses were almost certainly in China during the reign of Chin-nun (2737-2697 BC). Later, Emperor Wu Di (140-86 BC) extended rose growing from private gardens to ornamental parks. In the

Rose Tree

fifth century AD the poet Hsieh Lung-yin celebrated the planting of roses in front of his windows; and Lo-yang (AD 960-1279) had forty-one varieties in his gardens. It is thought that the ancient Egyptians planted roses in gardens, too, though there is no definite proof of this.

Records from around 384-322 BC reveal that roses were grown in Greek gardens and that some, such as the Gardens of Adonis, were specifically devoted to roses. About the same time, the pleasure-loving philosopher Epicurus created his own rose garden to provide himself with a constant supply of blooms and petals. Records have also survived from around 1100 BC indicating that Tiglath-Pileser of Assyria had formal gardens and parks with many plants and water features; and it is known that the Romans had their own rose gardens, mainly formal ones, described as being "perfumed with roses."

Following the collapse of the Roman Empire little was recorded about rose gardens for several centuries – except for those cultivated by monks and nuns for medicinal, culinary, and cosmetic purposes. One rose planted in such monastic gardens was almost certainly the Apothecary's Rose (*R. gallica officinalis*). However, a number of famous rose gardens are mentioned in medieval documents. In sixth-century France Childebert I created a rose garden in Paris; in the eighth century the Emperor Charlemagne called for lilies and roses to be planted in the civic gardens of Aachen, in Germany; and in 1272 Edward I of England, newly returned from a Crusade, ordered rose trees for the gardens of the Tower of London. It was also during this period that the Moors planted a splendid rose garden in Cordoba, in Spain.

Oldest living roses

There is no doubt that the oldest known rose plant in the world today is the Rose of Hildesheim, a form of *R. canina* (the Dog Rose) growing on one of the walls of the cathedral in Hildesheim, in Germany. It is believed to have been planted in AD 815 on the orders of Emperor Charlemagne – and, although damaged by fire during the Second World War, has nevertheless continued to flourish.

In the garden of Countess Nanda d'Ursel, in Belgium, three China roses (*R. chinensis* 'Multipetala', 'Old Blush', and one unnamed variety), all planted between 1772 and 1784, still flower freely.

At the Rose Tree Inn in Tombstone, Arizona, there is an incredible example of *R. banksiae* ('Lady Banks Rose'), planted in 1885 by a Scottish lady immigrant. This remarkable rose has a trunk some 6ft (2m) thick, clambers over 8,000 square feet (295 square meters) of supports, and each April produces thousands of white blooms.

The world's largest rose tree
Planted in 1885 in Tombstone, Arizona, this amazing example of R. BANKSIAE has now spread to cover more than 8,000 square feet of patio and is still growing.

ROSE COLLECTORS

ROSES WERE AMONG THE PLANTS collected by early civilizations. For instance, King Sargon (2371-2316 BC) brought back "foreign trees, vines, figs, and roses" from Turkey to Akkadia. This exchange of plants, especially between East and West, ceased almost completely for several centuries during the Dark Ages, although travels within the Western world meant there was still some movement of roses from country to country.

In sixteenth-century India, to stock the gardens of the Mogul emperors, numerous rose plants were imported from China, via the Silk Route, and also from Persia. From the late-eighteenth century onwards, plants from China were shipped to Europe, via Calcutta, by the East India Company. Among the roses sent to the West were 'Slater's Crimson China' (often called the 'Daily Rose' in America); *R. roxburghii* ('Chestnut Rose'), named after Dr. William Roxburgh, superintendant of the Calcutta Botanic Gardens; 'Hume's Blush Tea-Scented China'; 'Parks' Yellow Tea-Scented China', named after John Parks of the Royal Horticultural Society; the Climbers *R. banksiae* and *R. banksiae lutea* ('Yellow Banksian'); and 'Fortune's Double Yellow', found by botanist Robert Fortune. Other plant hunters included E. H. Wilson, who discovered species such as *R. helenae* (named after his wife) and *R. moyesii* and *R. davidii*, both of which have fantastic hips; Frank N. Meyer from America, who discovered *R. xanthina* and *R. x spontanea* ('Canary Bird'); and Dr. Max Wichura, who found *R. wichuraiana* in Japan.

The Empress Josephine
One of the most avid "collectors" was the Empress Josephine, wife of Napoleon, who sent scouts all over the world to find new roses. The result was a beautiful garden at Malmaison, near Paris, where she grew more than 250 varieties. Inevitably they cross-pollinated, but no records of the resulting hybrids were kept and rosarians such as Graham Stuart Thomas are still endeavoring to classify many of the roses grown there.

CHAPTER II

ROSES FOR YOUR GARDEN

THE ROSE IS FAIREST WHEN 'TIS BUDDING NEW,
AND HOPE IS BRIGHTEST WHEN IT DAWNS FROM FEARS;
THE ROSE IS SWEETEST WASHED WITH MORNING DEW,
AND LOVE IS LOVELIEST WHEN EMBALMED IN TEARS.
FROM "THE LADY OF THE LAKE" BY SIR WALTER SCOTT 1771-1832

GARDEN ROSES

LTHOUGH MANY OF THE EARLIEST ROSES evolved naturally, it is thought that artificial hybridization was carried out by the Chinese and possibly by other ancient peoples, too. However, this was probably done on a fairly random basis, and if any records were kept they would appear to have been lost.

This is why a certain amount of confusion exists concerning the correct name and origin of some roses. Moreover, natural variations occur from time to time – so, despite the careful records kept by modern hybridists, there is no knowing when the discovery of a new rose may be just around the corner.

The nineteenth century saw the beginning of the serious, scientific breeding of roses, which produced the roses of today.

MARÉCHAL NIEL
A nineteenth-century variety of the Noisette group. This was an early success in producing a yellow hybrid from China Roses.

22

R. GALLICA

AUSTRIAN YELLOW (R. FOETIDA)

Old roses

Certain of the old roses had proved particularly valuable for breeding – namely *R. gallica* (the French Rose), *R. alba* (meaning "white rose"), and the repeat-flowering 'Autumn Damask' (a form of *R. damascena*), which were already being grown in gardens in Europe during the sixteenth century. These were eventually joined by *R. centifolia* (the Cabbage Rose), 'Austrian Yellow' (a form of *R. foetida* from Persia), and *R. moschata* (the Musk Rose) from Northern India. Towards the end of the eighteenth century various roses, known collectively as China Roses, were imported into Europe from China. In Victorian times, Tea Roses also found their way to the West from China and were used for breeding purposes. A further rose that came to the West in the mid nineteenth century was *R. multiflora*, from Japan, which is one of the parents of many of the multi-flowered modern roses.

CHAPEAU DE NAPOLEON (CENTIFOLIA)

COMTE DE CHAMBORD (PORTLAND)

GLOIRE DE DIJON (NOISETTE)

FERDINAND PICHARD (BOURBON x HP)

ULRICH BRUNNER (HYBRID PERPETUAL)

Portland Roses

In the nineteenth century, by crossing roses from the Orient with those from the West, new groups were developed. Among these were the Portland Roses, though few of them now remain.

Noisette Roses

Noisette Roses were introduced about the same time in South Carolina, and some of these Ramblers are still to be found in catalogs today.

Bourbon Roses

Perhaps the biggest breakthrough of the nineteenth century was the creation of Bourbon Roses. Earlier roses produced blooms only once in a season, but the Bourbons flowered repeatedly. They are said to have originated from a chance cross between 'Old Blush China' and 'Autumn Damask' on the Ile de Bourbon (now Réunion) in the Indian Ocean. These roses were immensely popular and many varieties were introduced.

Hybrid Perpetuals

In the second half of the nine-teenth century, the Bourbons were surpassed by the Hybrid Perpetuals, thought to have originated from a cross between a Bourbon Rose and a Portland Rose. However, it was not long before elements of all the earlier groups – Hybrid Chinas and Noisettes, as well as Portlands and Bourbons – were involved in a great wave of breeding in America and the UK. It is reported that more than 3,000 varieties were raised and that the color range included pinks, mauves, purples, reds, and whites. It is still possible to find some of these varieties listed in rose catalogs.

Rosa Sulfurea. *Rosier jaune de soufre.*

R. SULFUREA
From LES ROSES by
**Pierre-Joseph Redouté
(1759-1840)**
*This was one of the first
yellow roses to reach
the West, around 1600,
from central Asia.*

25

PEACE (HYBRID TEA)

DOUBLE DELIGHT (HYBRID TEA)

PRISTINE (HYBRID TEA)

Hybrid Tea Roses

Although the groups already described represented important developments in rose breeding, nevertheless they left something to be desired so far as compactness of growth and reliable repeat flowering were concerned. Rose breeders therefore looked for ways of improving these aspects, and the result was the crossing of Hybrid Perpetuals with the smaller Tea Roses. 'La France', introduced by Jean-Baptiste Guillot in 1867, is thought to have been the first Hybrid Tea. Although this new group was not particularly popular initially, by the end of the nineteenth century there were some excellent varieties, many of which are still grown today.

The great breakthrough of Hybrid Teas was the production by the French Pernet-Ducher nursery of 'Soleil d'Or', which was the result of crossing a red Hybrid Perpetual with 'Persian Yellow' (*R. foetida persiana*). This was to become the ancestor of all sorts of beautiful yellow and orange roses – but it took the Pernet-Ducher family another ten years to breed a pure-yellow Hybrid Tea, which was named 'Rayon d'Or'.

Since 1910 many thousands of Hybrid Tea Roses have been developed, but perhaps one of the most unusual landmarks was the launching of a rose bred by Francis Meilland that was remarkable for the vigor of its growth and for its shapely high-centered form. This was smuggled out of France in 1940 by the last plane to the USA before the fall of France. It is known by a variety of names ('Mme A. Meilland' in France, 'Gloria Dei' in Germany, and 'Gioia' in Italy), but in America it was suggested that it should be called 'Peace' and the name was officially announced in 1945 on the day that Berlin fell.

Polyanthas

While the development of Hybrid Teas, with their single-stemmed flowers, was taking place, other breeders were endeavoring to produce a rose with clusters of blooms. Eventually, Jean-Baptiste Guillot crossed *R. multiflora* with a China Rose, and so were born the Polyantha Roses.

Poulsen Roses

By the early twentieth century the Polyantha Roses were already popular; but to improve them still further, the Danish Poulsen family crossed some Polyanthas with Hybrid Teas, thus creating, in 1924, a new group that became known as the Poulsen Roses.

Floribundas

As more and more hybridists got to work in the United States, France, Germany, Denmark, Britain, and other countries, the influence of the Hybrid Tea became more marked, and the various types of cluster-flowered hybrids became collectively known as Floribundas – originally an American name that was accepted universally in the 1950s. Another term introduced about the same time in the USA was Grandiflora, signifying roses with the tall Floribunda growth habit and trusses of blooms that have high centers similar to those of Hybrid Teas. Among the early Grandifloras were 'Queen Elizabeth' and 'Pink Parfait'.

BETTY PRIOR (FLORIBUNDA)

QUEEN ELIZABETH (GRANDIFLORA)

POLYANTHA (GRANDIFLORA)

27

PICASSO (FLORIBUNDA)

RISE 'N' SHINE (MINIATURE)

MODERN ROSES

New colorings

Breeders are constantly working to improve the health, vigor, color, and fragrance of the two main groups of modern roses – the Hybrid Teas and Floribundas – while at the same time introducing new types. In fact, there are now roses in all colors (including green), with the exception of a true blue – and it may not be too long before that is introduced, too. Thanks to Sam McGredy (from the long-established Irish rose-growing family, who moved his nursery to New Zealand in the 1970s) there are also bi-colored roses. These followed from his introduction of a red-and-white Floribunda, 'Picasso', in 1971.

Miniature & Patio Roses

The 1970s also saw the introduction of Miniature Roses, perfect replicas of their big brothers and sisters. These were followed by dwarf Shrub Roses, now generally (though unofficially) called Patio Roses. Both of these groups are ideal for small gardens, and quite a lot of people now concentrate on growing them to the exclusion of the taller varieties.

Ground-cover Roses

The late 1980s witnessed the advent of genuine low-growing Ground-cover Roses, specially bred to spread without gaining height. Incidentally, these make wonderful hanging basket displays. Also beginning to make their presence felt are Climbing Miniatures and Climbing Patio Roses, which will no doubt prove equally popular.

SUNNY (PATIO)

English Roses

Another recent group of roses fast becoming popular are David Austin's English Roses, described by him as "new roses in the old tradition."

These are the outcome of hybridizing modern varieties with Old Roses. The result has been a combination of the recurrent-flowering habit and large color range of the Modern Roses with the characteristic flower formation, fragrance, and charm of the Old Roses.

English Roses are classified as Shrub Roses, but have yet to be included in the official classification table. For the sake of simplicity, these interesting new hybrids are included among the Old Garden Roses in the table on pages 30-1.

GRAHAM THOMAS (ENGLISH ROSE)

CLASSIFICATION OF ROSES

NAMES SUCH AS HYBRID TEAS AND FLORIBUNDAS are widely used throughout the world. However, as more and more new varieties appeared, rosarians felt that a more precise and logical form of classification was needed. As a result, in 1971 the World Federation of Rose Societies accepted proposals for improved classification put forward by the British members of the WFRS. This is very gradually being adopted in gardening books and specialist catalogs, but it may be many more years before it is accepted universally.

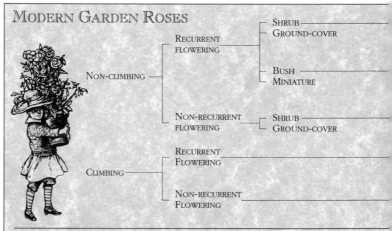

MODERN GARDEN ROSES

NON-CLIMBING
— RECURRENT FLOWERING
— SHRUB
— GROUND-COVER
— BUSH
— MINIATURE
— NON-RECURRENT FLOWERING
— SHRUB
— GROUND-COVER

CLIMBING
— RECURRENT FLOWERING
— NON-RECURRENT FLOWERING

OLD GARDEN ROSES

NON-CLIMBING

CLIMBING

A rose arbor laden with abundant Climbers

The rose renamed
The classification table below is essentially that used by the WFRS, but the Grandiflora, Ground-cover, Climbing Miniature, and Patio groups have been included, too. Officially, Hybrid Teas have become Large-flowered Roses; Floribundas are now Cluster-flowered Roses; and Patio Roses are classified as Dwarf Cluster-flowered Roses (perhaps too much of a mouthful ever to catch on?).

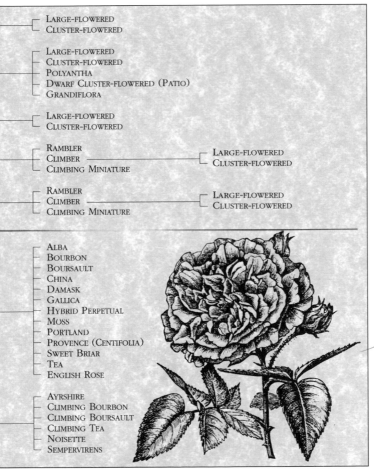

- LARGE-FLOWERED
- CLUSTER-FLOWERED

- LARGE-FLOWERED
- CLUSTER-FLOWERED
- POLYANTHA
- DWARF CLUSTER-FLOWERED (PATIO)
- GRANDIFLORA

- LARGE-FLOWERED
- CLUSTER-FLOWERED

- RAMBLER
- CLIMBER ——— LARGE-FLOWERED / CLUSTER-FLOWERED
- CLIMBING MINIATURE

- RAMBLER
- CLIMBER ——— LARGE-FLOWERED / CLUSTER-FLOWERED
- CLIMBING MINIATURE

- ALBA
- BOURBON
- BOURSAULT
- CHINA
- DAMASK
- GALLICA
- HYBRID PERPETUAL
- MOSS
- PORTLAND
- PROVENCE (CENTIFOLIA)
- SWEET BRIAR
- TEA
- ENGLISH ROSE

- AYRSHIRE
- CLIMBING BOURBON
- CLIMBING BOURSAULT
- CLIMBING TEA
- NOISETTE
- SEMPERVIRENS

31

CREATING HYBRIDS

BASICALLY HYBRIDIZING IS EXTREMELY SIMPLE – merely use the pollen from one rose and transfer it to the stigma of another, then sow the resulting seeds and grow the plants. But the likelihood of producing a "winner" by this method is remote, and most hybridizers work to a very carefully planned breeding program.

Professionals first remove the petals from the seed parent, and then the stamens before they begin to shed pollen. The pollen from the selected pollinating parent is then brushed on to the stigmas of the female parent. If this is done in the open, the blooms have to be covered with paper bags to prevent any pollination from an unwanted source. In greenhouses, this practice is rarely necessary. The fertilized bloom is then labeled, generally with a code or some kind of abbreviation. The crosses are harvested in the fall, and the seeds stored until late winter. For germination, a cool temperature is required.

The resulting plants will flower the first summer, and this is when professionals start weeding out seedlings of poor quality. This culling and trial testing of new roses can take many years, so it may be some time before the results of the breeder's labors reach the market place.

The "father" of this method of rose breeding was Henry Bennett, who introduced his "pedigree" roses in Britain in 1878. Bennett kept careful records of the parentage of his hybrids, and their qualities proved beyond doubt that his method was preferable to random crossing.

Creating a hybrid
This is the method pioneered by Henry Bennett in the 1870s. Pollen from a selected pollinating parent is brushed onto the stigmas of the female parent.

Introducing new roses

Naming new roses

Given the number of new roses being introduced each year, there was clearly an ever-increasing risk of names being duplicated. Equally, the name given to a rose in its country of origin sometimes proved awkward, or even unpronounceable, in another language. The result could be confusing – for example, Kordes's 'Iceberg' is sold as 'Schneewittchen' in Germany and as 'Fée des Neiges' in France. To overcome these difficulties, many breeders, particularly in Europe, now use a system of coding, each new rose being given an "official" name based on the breeder's own name. For example, the rose called 'Elina' in America and 'Peaudouce' in Britain is officially known as Dicjana – which identifies it internationally as having been bred by Dickson of Northern Ireland.

Rose trials

It always helps to establish a new variety if the breeder can claim that it has received national or international awards after stringent tests. These trials are generally organized by the various national rose societies – especially in America, Europe, and Japan – and the results are published in their journals annually.

The AARS (All-America Rose Selections), for example, has more than twenty official test gardens throughout the United States, so new roses can be assessed over a two-year period under widely varying conditions. (In most instances, the roses will also undergo a four-year trial period in the breeder's own nursery.) Once the awards have been announced, the roses are marketed the following year and publicized in some 150 public gardens.

Another type of trial is conducted by the American Rose Society, which produces an annual survey of the top thirty roses. Called "Proof of the Pudding," it is published in the Society's journal and is a useful guide for gardeners trying to decide which are the best roses to grow.

Roses for Every Garden

THE MOTTO OF THE AMERICAN ROSE SOCIETY IS "A rose in every home, a bush in every garden" – and nowadays there is such an enormous choice of varieties available, with such a wide range of characteristics, that the rose is even more versatile than before.

Roses can be used for hedging, especially *R. rugosa* varieties, which produce handsome decorative hips after flowering. Most of the old and modern Shrub Roses require a fair amount of space, but are most effective in larger gardens. Hybrid Teas and Floribundas are best grown in beds on their own, or with carefully selected companion plants. Climbers and Ramblers need height to give of their best and can be supported by wires, trellises, trees, or other supports, such as pergolas and arches, thus creating an attractive garden feature. Ground-cover Roses, as their name implies, are prostrate growers, and some are nearly evergreen, so act as weed-suppressors.

With gardens becoming ever smaller, it is not surprising that Miniatures and Patio Roses have become so popular. Patio Roses are generally defined as varieties that reach a height of 1½-2ft (45-60cm), while Miniatures are ones that do not exceed 1½ft (45cm). Indeed, some Miniatures attain a height of only 6in (15cm). Breeders in America were the first to see the great potential of these "dwarfs" and have bred vast numbers of varieties in a wide range of colors and bi-colors.

Miniatures and Patio Roses grow well in raised beds and containers, and generally require the same care as larger roses. If they are grown in containers, extra feeding, watering, and frost protection are needed.

Roses for hedges
R. RUGOSA has a well-deserved reputation for resistance to disease, as well as for its attractive hips and tough wrinkled leaves. It has a very long flowering season and requires little maintenance.

CHAPTER

III

ROSES IN LORE & ART

*THE ROSE HAS ONE POWERFUL VIRTUE TO BOAST
ABOVE ALL THE FLOWERS OF THE FIELD:
WHEN ITS LEAVES ARE ALL DEAD, AND FINE COLOURS ARE LOST,
STILL HOW SWEET A PERFUME
IT WILL YIELD!*
FROM "THE ROSE" BY ISAAC WATTS 1674-1748

The symbolic rose

MOST CULTURES HAVE MYTHS OR LEGENDS involving roses. The rose, the myrtle, and the apple were sacred to the Greek goddess of love, Aphrodite – or Venus as the Romans called her. Red roses were said to have sprung from the drops of blood that fell on the ground when Aphrodite pricked herself on some thorns. Roses were also present at the birth of Venus: when she emerged from the sea, standing on a scallop shell, they were said to have rained from the sky. Another Greek legend is that Rhodanthe, Queen of Corinth, sought refuge in the temple of Diana. So beautiful was she that people began to worship her instead of the goddess. To avenge this insult, Diana's brother, Apollo, turned Rhodanthe into a rose bush, and her three suitors into a butterfly, a worm, and a fly.

According to Islamic tradition, roses were the droplets of sweat formed when the prophet Mohammed perspired. Alternatively, the white rose was created after the flowers complained that the lotus slept at night; then, when a nightingale fell in love with the rose, during an embrace the bird's breast was pricked by a thorn and its blood turned the white flowers red.

One medieval legend told how a girl unjustly condemned to be burnt at the stake was saved when the flames were transformed into red and white roses. And it was said that in the Garden of Eden the white rose blushed and turned red after being kissed by Eve.

Heraldry

The ancient Greeks and Romans used the rose as a heraldic symbol. Coins from the island of Rhodes dated 400 BC, for example, have a rose motif stamped on one side. However, the rose is perhaps most closely linked with the British royal family. The first English monarch to use it as his device was Edward I, who chose a gold rose; Henry IV used a red rose; Edward IV a white one within a circle of sun rays. But it was the Tudors who really made the rose their own symbol, adopting a stylized form with a white rose placed in the center of a red rose, often surmounted by a crown. More recently, in 1986, the rose was adopted as the floral emblem of the United States.

THE MIRACLE OF SAINT BERNARD
Daniel Segbers and Erasmus Quellinus, c. 1625
In the Middle Ages the rose became a symbol of purity and goodness.
This Dutch painting contains a number of roses in the border.

Religion

Because the Virgin Mary was closely associated with the rose, the flower become a symbol of purity and Christian virtue. Red roses were seen as symbolizing the Virgin's sorrow, white roses her joy, and gold roses her glory.

According to Christian tradition, the rosary – which was the Virgin Mary's gift to Saint Dominic – was either made from rose petals or scented with roses. In more modern times, in Saint Bernadette's vision at Lourdes the Virgin appeared from a circle of roses.

In Christian symbolism roses are perhaps above all associated with Christ's wounds and the crown of thorns. They are also associated with many of the saints and with the blood of Saint Dorothy and other martyrs.

In the Old Testament there are several apparent references to roses, but most experts now argue that they are the product of mistranslation.

The Wars of the Roses

The Wars of the Roses, the prolonged power struggle that took place in England in the fifteenth century, were said to have started when a member of the House of York plucked a white rose (possibly *R. x alba semi-plena*) as his emblem and the rival House of Lancaster chose a red rose (*R. gallica officinalis*). The Tudor rose represented the reconciliation of the two warring factions, with the marriage of Henry Tudor (Henry VII) to Elizabeth of York.

R. ALBA x SEMI-PLENA

R. GALLICA OFFICINALIS

CHOOSING THE RED AND WHITE ROSES IN THE TEMPLE GARDENS
Henry A. Payne (1868-1939)
This superbly executed watercolor painting depicts the choosing of the rose symbols by the opposing Houses of York and Lancaster. The photos (above) show the species believed to have been chosen.

38

The rose in art

Pictures of roses can be divided into two categories – those done for botanical purposes and those in which the artist's purpose is not primarily scientific. In this latter group there are many artists who portrayed roses remarkably accurately – not least the great Flemish flower painters of the sixteenth and seventeenth centuries, of whom Jan ("Velvet") Brueghel is possibly the best known. His paintings and those of contemporary artists were incredibly lifelike, often including dewdrops and insects for further realism.

Prior to this period, artists such as the Italian Sandro Botticelli frequently used the rose as an object of beauty in their paintings. Botticelli's *The Birth of Venus*, *The Coronation of the Virgin and Saints*, and *Primavera* all include roses. Two superb examples of Spanish paintings depicting roses are Murillo's *Flower Girl* and Velázquez's *Coronation of the Virgin.*

Among botanical artists, the most celebrated painter of roses is undoubtedly Pierre-Joseph Redouté. Before Redouté, other French, Italian, German, Flemish, and Dutch artists had made drawings or paintings of roses to illustrate herbals and other books. Among the best known are the della Robbias, van Eyck, Memling, Dodoens, and Fuchs. Their illustrations were often copied in later works, such as John Gerard's *Herball* published in 1597.

More recently, in Victorian times and the twentieth century, there have been a number of outstanding modern botanical artists – but perhaps none as brilliant as Alfred Parsons, who illustrated Ellen Willmott's *Genus Rosa*, published shortly before the First World War.

R. Hollandica
Woodcut illustration from the Herball *of John Gerard, 1597. Gerard wrote enthusiastically about the rose, extolling it for "his beautie, vertues, and his flagrant and odiferous smell."*

R. INDICA FRAGRANS (BENGAL ROSE)

Pierre-Joseph Redouté

The magnificent three-volume LES ROSES by Redouté is much reproduced today, and has been of great assistance in identifying early roses. His patron was the Empress Joséphine, and his paintings were extremely popular during his lifetime. The illustration above is his study of R. INDICA FRAGRANS (the Bengal Rose).

THE ROSE AS ORNAMENT

IT IS THOUGHT THAT the earliest use of the rose for decorative purposes was the rosette motif, which existed in Mediterranean countries as long ago as 3000 BC and was widely used in Roman times. The rose appears as a romantic symbol in Roman jewelry, carving, and metalwork and also in early ceramics and enamels. In Islamic countries, the flowers frequently figure in architectural ornamentation and in embroideries and carpets.

Perhaps one of the most delightful symbolic uses of the rose is the beautiful stained-glass rose windows that are found in medieval cathedrals and churches from the twelfth century onwards.

The Tudor rose (see HERALDRY, page 36) was used by the London Pewterers' Company during the sixteenth and seventeenth centuries, together with a crown, as a symbol of quality. This may possibly be why so many public houses in Britain are called "The Rose & Crown."

In the late seventeenth and early eighteenth centuries, it was highly fashionable to incorporate the rose as an ornament in furniture designs – as a carving or in inlay work or, a little later, in painted designs. Similar forms of decoration were applied to musical instruments, too.

Roses appear particularly frequently in tapestries and other forms of embroidery, and feature regularly as motifs in all sorts of textiles – including lace, silks, wallcoverings, illuminated vellums, and painted fans.

The rose is particularly lovely when used decoratively on glass. There are beautiful seventeenth-century Jacobite glasses engraved with heraldic roses; and later, in the eighteenth century, roses were a popular form of decoration on candlesticks, vases, bottles, and other kinds of glass. In the mid nineteenth century, the French

Rose china
Early-twentieth-century bone-china cup and saucer with transfer rose design – the epitome of genteel living.

Rose cameo
*Late-Victorian pendant, hand-painted
on porcelain. It has a retaining ring
for a photograph or lock of hair.*

Clichy and Baccarat factories produced exquisite floral paperweights, and those featuring colored roses were much sought after as collector's pieces.

Porcelain has always provided a means of employing the rose decoratively to great advantage, and from the mid eighteenth century onwards ceramic ornaments and tableware were produced by many famous factories, such as Meissen, Sèvres, Derby, and Coalport. Sometimes the rose is enameled, sometimes painted, and sometimes modeled – but in whatever form it is used, porcelain with rose designs is now eagerly collected.

Through the ages jewelers have made frequent use of the rose, both as a motif and in realistic form. Roses have been created in enamel, gold, silver, and pearls – and remarkably realistic flowers have been fashioned from rubies and diamonds. The American designer Louis Comfort Tiffany and the Russian Carl Fabergé both produced some particularly magnificent jewelry and *objets d'art* inspired by the rose. Today, one of the most popular gems is the rose-cut diamond, having up to twenty-four facets to give it extra brilliance.

Rose souvenir
*Intricate turn-of-the-century rose
brooch – a superb example of Italian
glass mosaicwork. This type of jewelry was
extremely popular and was often brought
back home by tourists as a souvenir.*

43

THE ROSE IN POETRY

THE ROSE IN POETRY goes back to classical times. As mentioned earlier, Homer talks about roses in *The Iliad* and it was probably the Greek poetess Sappho who first called the rose "The Queen of Flowers." Since then, the flower has been a favorite topic with poets in practically every age.

Pierre de Ronsard, the sixteenth-century French poet, was perhaps the first to do the rose full justice. Indeed, Mary Queen of Scots, who loved roses and included them in her needlework, was so enamored of Ronsard's poetry that she sent him a silver rose as a mark of admiration. Earlier, Chaucer in his verse translation of the *Roman de la Rose* had helped to establish the rose as a symbol of romance, as had the Italian poet Dante in his effusions to his beloved Beatrice and in *The Divine Comedy*.

The rose has continued to supply images and themes for poems right up to the present day. Among the best known are Henry Lawes's "Gather ye rosebuds while ye may" and Robert Burns's "O, my Luve's like a red red rose." Rose gardens have been celebrated in verse, too, as witness Thomas Edward Brown's immortal lines:

> *A garden is a lovesome thing, God wot!*
> *Rose plot, Fringed pool, Ferned grot . . .*

Symbol of romance
In the nineteenth century the rose reached its zenith as a symbol of romantic love with the arrival of the printed Valentine card, and became almost an essential ingredient – although the quality of the verses often left something to be desired.

THE ROSE IN MUSIC

THE ROSE IN MUSIC AND LYRICS has a no less romantic connotation than the rose in poetry. Thomas Moore's famous *Selection of Irish Melodies*, for example, includes several songs about roses, among them "'Tis the Last Rose of Summer." This was inspired by a fine specimen of 'Parson's Pink China', one of the original China Roses introduced into Europe in the late eighteenth century.

"Rose"
A song sheet from the 1920s with a sentimental rose-inspired lyric.

Equally well known is "The Rose of Tralee" – and a rose of that name was intoduced by Sam McGredy in the 1960s. The original "rose" was a hat-shop assistant named Mary O'Sullivan, with whom William Mulchinock, the writer of the song, fell hopelessly in love.

In America, two highly popular lyrics immediately spring to mind. The first is Frank Lebby Stanton's sentimental song:

> *Sweetes' li'l' feller –*
> *Everybody knows;*
> *Dunno what ter call 'him*
> *But he's mighty lak' a rose!*

The second one is "The Yellow Rose of Texas," the ballad written in honor of Emily Morgan who helped the Texans win their freedom from Mexico – but, although the song and the story behind it are so well known, surprisingly there appears to be no rose bearing this name.

The rose often crops up in popular classical music, too, inspiring compositions such as Richard Strauss's *Der Rosen Kavalier*.

45

THE HERBAL ROSE

Although the very first medicinal uses of roses undoubtedly go back much further (to at least 5000 BC), Dioscorides's herbal written in the first century AD is probably the earliest book that gives details. According to Dioscorides, the hips of the Dog Rose *(R. canina)* – so called because the root was supposed to cure rabies – had innumerable medical uses. The crushed fruits were a cure for "stopping a loose belly and the spitting of blood." They could also

A visit to the apothecary
The pharmacists of the Middle Ages used rose hips and petals in many of their preparations.

be used as an eye salve and as a remedy for headaches, earache, toothache, "ye pains of ye seat," bladder disorders, and many other complaints. He also suggested that balls of dried rose petals should be used to combat the unsavory smell of sweat. The Roman writer Pliny repeats much of this information, but adds that rose petals in wine delay drunkenness and that Roman ladies thought the petals were effective for preserving beauty and youth.

In the Middle Ages, when roses were grown primarily in monastery gardens, they were used to make all sorts of salves, lotions, and medicines. In those days, rose petals were generally believed to have a purifying effect against diseases such as the plague, and people often carried nosegays of roses to freshen foul air.

R. canina (the Dog Rose)
Medieval apothecaries believed that the Dog Rose could cure all sorts of complaints.

ROSES IN COOKING

WHEN USING ROSE PETALS for any culinary purpose or for making wine, always make sure that they haven't been sprayed with garden chemicals. Also, always remove the base of the petals (the part where the petal joins the stalk).

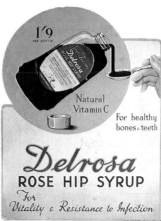

Rose-petal decorations

Crystalized rose petals are delightful decorations for desserts. Dip the petals in a stiff egg-white mixture, then in caster sugar, and place them on greaseproof paper on a baking tray.

Roses for health
During the Second World War rose-hip syrup was found to have a very high vitamin C content and was commonly given to babies.

(A pair of fine tweezers is useful for doing this.) Dry them in an airing cupboard, then store between layers of greaseproof paper in an airtight tin.

Fresh rose petals have a culinary use, too. They make attractive and unusual garnishes for many dishes, and are particularly pleasing in salads. Wash the petals gently before using them.

Rose-petal jam

Rose-petal jam is delicious and easy to make. Boil ¼ pint (150ml) of water, plus two tablespoons of orange juice and two of lemon juice, together with 1lb (500gm) of fine white sugar, until the mixture becomes syrupy. Add 4 ounces (100gm) of washed and dried red or pink rose petals, finely chopped, and simmer gently for about 30 minutes, stirring all the time. Pour into a small sterilized pot and seal.

Rose-hip jelly

Rose-hip jelly is made in a similar manner, but first of all you need to boil the hips to form a pulp and strain the juice from it through a jelly bag or fine sieve.

THE PERFUMED ROSE

R ECORDS INDICATE THAT ROSE PERFUME and rose water (made by steeping fragrant petals in boiling water) were in use more than 2,000 years ago. Nevertheless, exactly how the perfume was made does not appear to have been recorded until the nineteenth century, when the commercial production of perfumes commenced in France. Traditionally, various solvents and pure alcohol were used to extract the perfume from the petals of scented roses. Nowadays, however, it is more usual for chemicals to be blended together to create synthetic rose perfumes, although real roses are still used in the production of composite floral fragrances.

The discovery of attar of roses (rose oil) is traditionally attributed to Avicenna, the famous Arab physician and philosopher, in the eleventh century. However, it is quite possible that the Chinese were extracting oil many centuries earlier, and some sources attribute the discovery to Princess Nur Jahan, wife of the Mogul emperor Jahangir. She is said to have asked for the oil floating on the surface of her rose bath to be skimmed off, and when this was done it was found to be highly fragrant.

True attar of roses is such a concentrated perfume that it takes some 10,000 roses of suitable fragrance to produce about a third of a fluid ounce (10cl). It is still made by distillation in Bulgaria, India, and a number of Arab countries. Not surprisingly, true attar is a product for the very rich, although subsequent distillations of the Arab rose-water by-product are more reasonably priced. The rose used for making attar is usually 'Kazanlik' (a variety of *R.* x *damascena trigintipetala*), but experiments with other varieties are currently being conducted in Britain.

Potpourri

Originally a French term, "potpourri" has been part of the English language since the early seventeenth century. It is made by mixing together dried petals of sweet-scented roses and other flowers, which are then put into decorative bowls or sachets.

Medicinal potpourri was certainly made in the fifteenth century, and possibly earlier, as a means of combating

disease – the mixture of dried flowers and aromatic herbs being burnt and carried from room to room to act as a disinfectant. Nowadays, however, potpourri is generally made or bought solely for its fragrance.

To make potpourri, pick strongly perfumed rose petals before the blooms are fully open – preferably early in the day, although it is important that they are not wet from rain or dew. Lay the petals on sheets of tissue paper or newspaper and place them in an airing cupboard or a slightly warm oven. Turn the petals from time to time, until they are completely dried.

Place the dried rose petals in bowls and add to them other fragrant dried flowers, such as heliotrope, carnations, and lavender. Dried leaves of herbs can also be added – for example, mint, sage, thyme, lemon verbena, scented geraniums, and bay. Some people like to add grated nutmeg, cloves, allspice, and dried grated orange and lemon rind to give "zest" to the potpourri.

Finally, mix the ingredients together, add some orris-root powder (obtainable from pharmacists) as a "fixer," and fill decorative bowls or sachets with your potpourri. Stir occasionally and, when the scent fades, add a potpourri reviver (also available from pharmacists). In about two years' time, make a fresh supply.

49

FLOWER ARRANGEMENTS

W HAT CAN BE MORE ATTRACTIVE in the home than a single perfect rose bloom in a specimen vase, a bowl
of exquisite roses at their peak, or a
small "posy" of Miniatures as
a centerpiece on a table?

To extend the life of cut
roses, pick them early in the
evening or morning, as
the buds are half open
then. Remove the lower
leaves and thorns, slit the
bottom 1in (3cm) of the
stems, and stand the roses
up to their necks in water for
several hours – or, better still,
overnight – before arranging
them in your chosen bowl or
vase. If you are using floral foam
to hold the stems in position, soak the block thoroughly
before use. To make the flowers last as long as possible,
add a cut-flower preservative to the water in the vase or
bowl and top up the water from time to time.

Hips also make very decorative arrangements and can
either be used in their natural state or sprayed with lac-
quer so that they will last longer.

How to dry roses

Roses will last almost indefinitely in mixed dried-flower
arrangements, provided that they are dried and handled
carefully. Cut the blooms when just opening and remove
the stems. Then put a layer of dry fine sand in a box or
tin, lay the flowers face upwards on this, and gently add
more fine sand until the blooms are completely covered
by at least 1in (3cm) of sand. Gently tap the container to
eliminate air pockets, then seal it and put it in a warm
place. After about three weeks, gently tip off the sand
(which can be used again after being dried in an oven). If
need be, remove sand from between the petals with a
paintbrush. Finally, insert a florist's wire into the base of
each bloom and cover the wire with green florist's tape.

Chapter

IV

Care and
Cultivation

*It will never rain roses; when we want
to have more roses we must plant more trees.*
from "The Spanish Gypsy" by George Eliot 1819-1880

SELECTION & PREPARATION

PROVIDED THEY HAVE SUITABLE GROWING CONDITIONS, roses should thrive for twenty years or more. It is therefore essential to select the right site for roses, choose suitable varieties, prepare the soil for them thoroughly, plant them with care, and look after them well. However, it is amazing how tough roses are, and with a little care and attention they will give pleasure for months every year.

Selecting roses

You will find it is helpful to visit a local nursery or rose garden before you buy, so you can see varieties that are suited to your soil and climate. The best time to plant is during the fall, though healthy, vigorous container-grown plants can be bought at any time of year.

If buying bare-root plants, choose those with three (rather than two or one) healthy stems and check that they have good tap roots and plenty of capillary rootlets. The plants should look plump and healthy overall. If purchasing roses by mail order, send in your order in good time so it will reach you early in the planting season.

Preparing a rose bed

It is advisable to prepare the ground at least one month before planting, so that the soil has time to settle. If the site has had roses in it previously, it may well be what is termed "rose sick." If this is the case, the soil should either be treated chemically or changed – using fresh soil from another part of the garden, so the new roses will not suffer any ill-effects. If the soil has not been used for growing roses, dig it deeply to get it into good condition to receive the new plants. This is best done by double digging, which is described in most general gardening books. When you dig the bed, if your soil is sandy or clayey, incorporate some organic matter, such as shredded bark, peat, well-rotted compost, or cocoa or cotton-seed hulls. Adequate drainage is important, so your aim should be to create a good friable (crumbly) soil, preferably of a slightly acid nature (pH 6.0-6.5). If this cannot be achieved, you may need to purchase some suitable soil to make your rose beds.

Planting roses

BEFORE PLANTING ROSES in your prepared bed or border, insert a stake where each plant is to go, in order to ensure correct spacing. Make up a planting mixture consisting of 50% soil and 50% moist peat, with a handful of bone meal per 2 gallon (8 liter) bucketful. If the roots are spreading out all around the bush, dig a round hole for the plant; but if they're all growing in the same direction, make the hole fan-shaped. Whichever shape seems most appropriate, always make sure the hole is big enough to avoid cramping the roots.

Traditional rose garden, with Hybrid Teas framed by vigorous Ramblers.

Bedding in the plant

Set the plant in position and work one or two handfuls of planting mixture around the roots. Then cover the roots with some garden soil, gently shake the plant to ensure that there are no air pockets, and firm it into position with your hands.

Work mixture around roots.

Next, fill up the hole to the correct level – up to the soil mark on the stem, so the soil level will be the same as when the plant was growing in the nursery or garden center. Tread lightly around the plant to firm it into position. Then loosen the surface with a hoe or fork. After planting, water the rose.

Tread lightly around plant.

SPACING FOR ROSES

WHEN PLANTING RAMBLERS OR CLIMBERS against a wall, make sure they are at least 18in (45cm) away from it – otherwise they may not be able to benefit sufficiently from rain. Standard Roses need staking. Insert the stake before planting, on the windward side of the hole. The top of the stake should be just below the head of the tree. After planting, attach tree supports to anchor it to the stake. On average, planting distances between roses should be as follows:

Hybrid Teas and Floribundas – 2ft (60cm)
Grandifloras – 3ft (1m)
Small Shrubs – 3ft (1m)
Large Shrubs – about 5ft (1.8m)
Standards – 4ft (1.3m)
Climbers – 7ft (2.3m)
Ramblers – 10ft (3.8m)
Miniatures – 9in (23cm)
Patio Roses – 1ft (30cm)
Ground-cover Roses – half the expected spread.

Correct spacing
The illustration shows the correct spacing for roses. If the plants are crowded too close-ly together, they won't grow well; if they are planted too far apart, that spoils the display.

LARGE SHRUBS
5ft (1.8m)

HYBRID TEAS &
FLORIBUNDAS 2ft (60cm)

General care

A T THE BEGINNING OF EACH SEASON, hoe your rose beds, rake up weeds, and remove dead leaves and other debris. Apply a rose fertilizer at the rate recommended by the manufacturer and hoe it in. Then add a 2-3in (about 5-8cm) layer of organic matter to the soil as a mulch, first making sure that the soil is moist; if it is dry, water before mulching. Suitable mulches include shredded bark, peat, well-rotted manure or garden compost, ground corn cobs, or cocoa or cotton-seed hulls.

Where moderate climatic conditions prevail, further feeding with fertilizer will be required just before the buds open in early summer. In places where three or four flushes of bloom are normal, feed before each flush. Also, to prevent strain on the bushes, deadhead spent blooms on Hybrid Teas, Floribundas, and Grandifloras by cutting them off two to three leaves down the stem. Do not deadhead roses that flower only once in the season or those that produce decorative hips.

CLIMBERS
7ft (2.3m)

STANDARDS
4ft (1.3m)

GRANDIFLORAS
3ft (1m)

PATIO ROSES
1ft (30cm)

SMALL SHRUBS 3ft (1m)

Roses & the weather

Additional feeds with a proprietary liquid fertilizer can be given during the season as a boost to growth generally. But refrain from feeding roses when the fall is imminent, since feeding encourages soft growth that could be damaged by frost.

Although roses are hardy and resilient plants, prolonged periods of below-zero temperatures can kill them. In areas where such conditions are likely to occur, they therefore need to be given some protection before cold spells set in. The most common method is first to prune back all long growths by half (pruning proper should be carried out in the spring), then mound up soil around the base to a height of 6-12in (15-30cm), using soil from another part of the garden. In really cold areas, it may be necessary to dig away the soil on one side and then tilt the plant over and cover it completely.

Another method of winter protection is to erect a barrier around each rose and fill the space with materials such as leaves, straw, shredded bark, newspaper, or other materials that are dry. If a mulching material is used, it can then be spread over the bed the following spring.

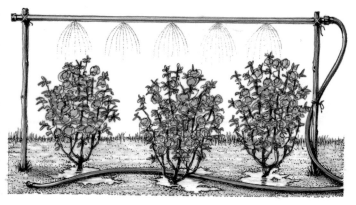

Growing roses in a hot climate
In many areas, and especially those with almost desert-like conditions, regular watering is essential. This is best done with an automatic trickle-irrigation system to the roots combined with an overhead spray line for evening spraying. If it is possible to fix some form of shade for the roses during the hottest part of the day, this will greatly assist the plants' vigor and will also help to reduce color fading of the blooms.

Pruning & Training

Unless roses are pruned regularly, they can soon become an untidy jumble of poor-quality stems and dead wood. The normal time for pruning Bush and Standard Roses is in the spring, just before the buds start into growth. For Ramblers and Climbers, different treatment is needed (see pages 58-9).

Correct pruning
Always prune just above a bud, sloping the cut downward.

Before pruning, always check that cutting tools – such as one-hand and long-handled pruners, pruning saw, and pruning knife – are sharp and will make good clean cuts. Make the cuts just above a bud, sloping downward away from it so that moisture will not get into the bud axil. Remove dead and diseased wood first; then cut out thin stems. Finally, prune the remainder to the required length.

Essential pruning tools
You will need one-hand pruners for light pruning and deadheading. A pruning knife is also useful. Thicker stems may need to be cut with long-handled pruners.

A newly planted Hybrid Tea *Pruned back to 6in stems*

Hybrid Teas, Floribundas, & Grandifloras

The first year after planting, Hybrid Teas, Floribundas, and Grandifloras need to be pruned to about 6in (15cm) above ground level. In subsequent years cutting stems back to about half their length gives good results, though for exhibition blooms harder pruning is needed.

Shrub, Miniature, Patio, & Ground-cover Roses

In their first year, Shrub, Miniature, Patio, and Ground-cover Roses need no pruning, and thereafter only require the removal of dead and spindly wood. (In the case of Miniatures, sharp scissors are the best pruning tools.)

Standards

The stems of Standard Roses, both ordinary and weeping, need cutting back after planting to 6-8in (15-20cm) from the top of the trunk. Thereafter, in spring moderately prune Hybrid Tea and Floribunda standards so that the stems are all about the same length and form a neat, well-balanced head that is not too heavy for the trunk.

Prune weeping standards in the fall, cutting out the old flowering wood and leaving young growths to produce blooms the following year.

Climbers

Climbers require little pruning at any time, apart from cutting out stems that are dead or spindly, or growing in the wrong direction, and shortening flowered wood. But

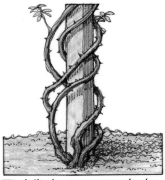

Wind Climber stems around pole   *Train Climber on fence into a fan*

Climbers do need training properly in order to give a good display. If grown up a pole, pergola, or arch, the stems should be twined around the supports and held in place with plastic-covered wire ties (but not too tightly, otherwise growth could be strangled). When Climbers are grown against a wall, fence, or other type of screen, the aim should be to get the stems to form a fan shape. This is done by tying the main stems to horizontal wire supports or to a trellis or other type of framework. This encourages lateral branches to appear that will grow upwards and produce blooms. These pruning and training methods may have to be varied slightly for certain varieties and different climatic conditions.

Ramblers

Ramblers, as their name implies, tend to climb freely up their supports. Therefore, unless they are being grown in a restricted space, they are best pruned very lightly, simply cutting out dead and old stems and tipping laterals that have flowered.

Ramblers grown in a confined space are best pruned in the fall. Cut out as many of the flowered stems as possible and tie in the new stems, which will bear flowers the following year. Cut back any lateral growths to about 3in (7-8cm). As with Climbers, the variety and climatic conditions will influence pruning methods. With a little experience, you will be able to judge how much wood to remove each year.

CONTAINER GROWING

GROWING ROSES IN CONTAINERS is becoming more and more popular, especially now smaller rose varieties are available. The great advantage of outdoor container cultivation is that you can grow plants where flower beds are lacking – on patios and balconies, for example. The roses can be planted, either singly or in groups, in tubs or troughs. When buying the roses and containers, it's worth choosing colors and textures that are complementary.

Growing roses in containers outdoors

Choose a container large enough for the type of rose to be grown – the depth needs to be 9in (20-25cm) for Miniatures, 12in (30cm) for Patio Roses, and 15in (35-40cm) for the smaller Hybrid Teas and Floribundas. Use a proprietary potting compost, and maintain the plants in a similar manner to roses grown in beds. A further advantage of container growing – especially useful if you live in a cold area – is that you can move the containers indoors for the winter so the plants will not be exposed to frost.

Flower pot.

Growing roses indoors

You can grow Miniatures indoors all the year round, but they need plenty of light and a humid atmosphere in order to thrive. The best method is to place the pots on a tray of gravel, which you will need to keep watered, and stand it in a sunny position. Spray the plants with water regularly, feed every two months, and expose them to fluorescent lighting during winter. Repot the plants each spring, using fresh compost.

60

PROPAGATION

Taking cuttings

Cuttings are easy to root – but in order to obtain plants that are vigorous, when you plant them out discard the weaker ones and retain only the strongest. Cuttings taken in late summer or fall can be rooted outdoors; for cuttings taken earlier in the year, you need propagating equipment and a greenhouse.

Generally, cuttings should be about 8in (20cm) long. Cut a current year's growth shoot off the selected rose, trim off top and bottom growth with a sloping cut, and remove all but the top two leaves. Place the cuttings in a sandy trench, with just the leaves above ground, and firm back the soil. In cold areas, cover the tops with protective material (see GENERAL CARE, page 55). The new plants will be ready for planting out about twelve months later.

Cuttings of Miniature and Patio Roses should be 3-4in (about 7-10cm) long and are best rooted in pots or growing bags in a frost-free situation.

Budding

Increasing roses by budding is much more complicated than taking cuttings and involves buying suitable rootstocks such as 'Laxa' or *R. multiflora*.

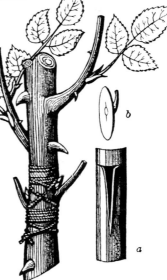

Plant these in late fall. Then around the middle of the following summer, scrape away the soil to expose the neck of the rootstock, make a T-cut with a sharp knife, and ease back the flaps of bark. Cut a shield-shaped piece of wood with a plump, healthy bud on it from the variety that is to be increased. Carefully remove the wood behind the bud, and insert the bud shield into the T-cut. Fix this in position with raffia or a proprietary tie.

Provided it has been properly protected from winter frosts, the new plant should be growing freely the following year. Once it is established, cut off the top of the rootstock carefully.

The art of budding
Illustration from THE ROSE GARDEN by William Paul, 1863. Successful budding takes skill, so ask someone experienced to demonstrate the technique before you try it.

ROSE TROUBLES

LIKE OTHER PLANTS, roses can be attacked by insects and fungi. If a plant's growth is healthy and vigorous, then it is much less likely to succumb to parasitic organisms – so it pays to look after roses well. Generally, the rule should be to spray insects as soon as you spot them and to spray fungus before it becomes visible.

All good gardening stores and garden centers stock a selection of proprietary rose insecticides and

BLACKFLY

fungicides. With all of them it is important to follow the manufacturer's instructions carefully and to spray the plants thoroughly, using a sprayer that is kept specifically for the purpose.

Always spray your roses in the evening, when bees and other beneficial insects are less likely to be around. Avoid applying chemicals when the leaves are wet and when the weather is very sunny or windy.

LEAF-ROLLING SAWFLY

Pests

Aphids (greenfly and blackfly), which are probably the most common pests, can often be controlled by a blast of plain water, as can froghoppers and spider mites. Other insects that attack roses include thrips, leafhoppers, caterpillars, leaf-rolling sawflies, and gall wasps. Systemic insecticides are useful for controlling most of these pests. Spraying with petroleum oil or lime sulfur during the dormant season may help, too.

Diseases

Watch out for blackspot, rust, powdery mildew, rose canker, and crown gall, which are the most common fungus diseases. You can deal with the first three by spraying affected plants with a systemic fungicide. But with rose canker and crown gall, it is necessary to cut out and burn all affected stems; if the plant is badly affected, the whole of it should be destroyed by burning.

Suckers

These also need to be dealt with, since they reduce the strength of the plant. Remove suckers by tracing them back to the roots and pulling them off.